PUPPY
IN MY HEAD

A BOOK ABOUT MINDFULNESS
ELISE GRAVEL

HARPER
An Imprint of HarperCollins Publishers

There is a puppy in my head. His name is

OLLiE.

Most of the time, Ollie is

QUiET.

He sits or sleeps. He's a good puppy.

Ollie is very

CURiOUS.

He wants to explore everything, smell everything, say hello to everybody, and go everywhere.

That's how puppies learn.

Sometimes, Ollie is all over the place. He gets

EXCiTED.

Then I get excited, too.

When he's happy-excited, it's fun.
I feel like jumping around or dancing.

But it's not fun when Ollie is too excited.
That's when he runs around in my head
and makes too much

He can't calm down.

I can't calm down, either.

Sometimes he gets

SCARED.

He tries to warn me that there is danger.
Most of the time, the danger is not real.

But then I get scared, too.

Eek! What is it, Ollie? Is there something we should be afraid of?

If I listened to him every time he got scared, I'd be scared a lot.

I try to tell him

AWOOO!

But it doesn't
always work.

He needs help to calm down.
It's not easy for a puppy.

If he gets too excited, scared, or upset, he can't listen to me. His

FEELiNGS

control him.

When that happens, I take out my magical

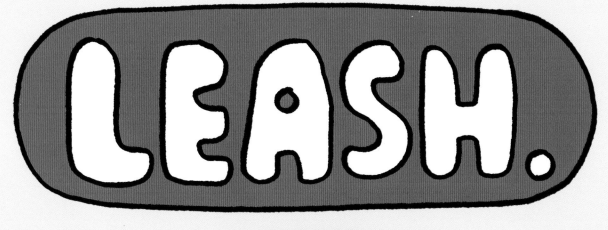

It's not a leash that you can see. It's invisible.
The leash is my

BREATH.

I sit down and take a deep breath.
Long, slow, and

GENTLE.

Then I breathe out, very

SLOWLY.

The sound of my breath calms Ollie.

He comes closer.

I breathe in and out a few more times . . .
as many times as it takes, but always

SLOWLY.

Ollie follows my breath and comes
to sit right next to me. We

CUDDLE.

It's okay, Ollie.

He's asleep now. See? He just needed

We're both feeling better now.

There are other ways I can help Ollie.

When he gets too excited, he needs to use up his

ENERGY.

I take him for a walk or a run

or to chase a ball.

Sometimes, Ollie just needs to talk. I listen and try to understand what he's telling me.

Then I can

TALK ABOUT iT

to someone, too.

Ollie is upset because I had a fight with my friend.

Mostly, what Ollie needs is for me to pay

ATTENTiON

and spend more time with him.

I love Ollie. He's such a good puppy.
He is my best

FRiEND.

EVERYBODY

has a puppy in their head. Even grown-ups.

DO YOU HAVE ONE?

WHAT IS YOUR PUPPY'S NAME?

For my daughters, Sophie and Marie, and
their imaginary puppy, Kleenex. —E.G.

It's very important to help our children learn the skills they need to manage anxiety and stress. **Puppy in My Head** is a lovely way to introduce mindfulness to children and parents: It's not only a step-by-step introduction to conscious breathing and a focused mind, but it also shows children that thoughts and feelings are things we can identify and understand. With awareness growing about the health impacts of toxic stress, books like this are brilliant at introducing children to mental health and mindfulness. We all have puppies in our heads, and with breathing and guidance, we can learn to calm them.

- Dr. Deirdre Bernard-Pearl
Pediatric Medical Director, Santa Rosa Community Health
Santa Rosa, California